A Faithful God

Lessons from the Pacific Crest Trail

Paul Volkov

A Faithful God: Lessons from the Pacific Crest Trail

Copyright © 2018 Paul Volkov. All rights reserved. No part of this book may be reproduced or retransmitted in any form or by any means without the written permission of the publisher.

Published by Twenty Miles a Day
Phoenix, Arizona

ISBN: 978-0-692-11850-4 (paperback)
ISBN: 978-0-692-12718-6 (ebook)
LCCN: 2018943481

rev201801

Contents

Preface and Introduction 1
1 Having Faith 3
2 Stepping out in Faith 9
3 Zero Day (So Soon?) 15
4 Having Your Own Faith 19
5 Navigational Faith 25
6 False Faith 33
7 Nero Day … Not a Full Zero 41
8 Sharing Faith 43
9 Perfect Vision Faith 47
10 Nutritional Faith 51
11 Another Nero! 57
12 Knowing Faith 59
13 Expecting Faith 65
14 Faith after Disillusionment 69
15 Shaking-the-Crud-off Faith 75
16 Winding It Up 79

Pacific Crest Trail

2,650 miles

Preface and Introduction

2 Corinthians 4:13 says, "I believed, therefore I spoke." That's exactly it. I believe! Therefore, I'm speaking—writing, actually. It's just a matter of semantics. I believe God wants His people, His children—you—to know Him better and for us to increase in our faith in Him in order to develop that most profound of relationships with Him, because He wants to be with us. That's His name, and that's His word to us—Immanuel—God with us.

This collection of concepts that I'm sharing is supposed to encourage you to believe and trust the Lord God in every aspect of your life. Encouraging you to grow your faith in Jesus and to grow in your faith so God's best, perfect, and pleasing plan will be—not just can be, *will be*—accomplished in you.

I'm just some ordinary guy who believes God told me to, "Share what you believe. My children need some encouragement. Just do it." To me, I'm the wrong guy. I don't feel qualified or even worthy or capable. I'm just a carpenter, but I believe God knows what He is doing and wants me to fulfill His purpose. So I'll take Him at His word. I'll just do it.

The steps to the faith that manifests the Glory of God and produces the physical evidence of things not seen and the substance of things hoped for (Heb. 11:1) have to start somewhere. They also have to continue. This encouragement is in faith that God will minister peace in your life, which will direct you to Him by a closer fellowship with Him that builds your faith and trust in God.

All this results from my experience on the Pacific Crest Trail in the spring of 2017. The Pacific Crest Trail does amazing things for every hiker who attempts it. Whether one completes it or not, it is prolific in its impact on one's life. No, I didn't complete it. But what an impact! And yes, my faith was tested, and it grew. God is good, and His word is true! Here's what I learned.

ONE

Having Faith

I gotta go with this …

So there I was, 10 miles into a 2,660-mile hike. The Pacific Crest Trail (PCT) goes from the United States' border with Mexico to Canada, through California, Oregon, and Washington. Just ten stinkin' miles on the PCT and my right ACL—a ligament on the outside of your knee—gave way to bitter pain and grief that I'd never known. My brother, the nurse, who was also hiking with me, checked it out and said, rather characteristically, "Yeah, that's your ACL. Sorry it hurts. Wanna use my poles?" Thanks, bro! C'mon! Ten miles? No, no, no. This can't be right! I expected more. This isn't what I told everybody. Like I'm gonna spend four months planning and pay out a couple grand for gear and supplies only to hike ten lousy miles? Uh-uh! No way!

With every painful step, I hobbled and

limped the next ten miles to the first campsite, using one of my brother's hiking poles. I argued within myself about the faith I needed, convinced that it needed to be stronger and wondering if, or how, I could increase my faith. "Is it an attack from the enemy? Is this really with God's approval? Am I presumptuous in saying this trip is a gift from the Lord God?" I bragged about this to all my family and my friends in church and to my coworkers. Yes, I planned for four months and trained and did all this work to get here, and now how am I to explain this failure?

Bless God for His love, mercy, and truth! I had to do a heap of praying, meditating on those verses of healing and God's love for me. Yes, it's just as difficult for me as anyone else to step out into a level of faith where I really need it and to continue with that same built-up faith that seems so unnatural. Although my reaction to my malady seems so generic ("Just pray and ask God," a typical mediocre response), that's the step I took toward my loving and promise-keeping God. God is real! He hears, He listens, and He answers! Fortunately for me, my brother left his medication at the home of our pretrail host in San Diego, who also drove us out to the trailhead/southern terminus earlier that day, which made us stay put at our campsite an extra day. The extra day was long enough for my communion with God through prayer to seek His direction. And bless God, our gracious host drove back out and delivered that medication to my brother the next day.

With abundant prayer and prayer over the phone with a pastor I know, God met me while I was floundering on the trail and spoke to me. Yes, God still speaks! We just need to be attentive. He said, "All right, I'm going to give you your daily steps. I'm already your daily bread. Now get up, start hiking, stop moaning, and move along. I will give you enough steps to get you to your next campsite and all those following." Really? As in, and without doubt, total amazement, and utter shock. God gave me my daily steps! He really did! When your ACL goes out, that's it. You just don't get to ignore it and keep going—that's it! But my God and loving Father chose differently. My Creator, who loves me that much, healed me and delivered me and gave me all I needed! I did the possible by believing; God did the impossible by hearing, listening, and healing.

The Lord God wanted me to know that He was right there with me. Deuteronomy 31:6 says, "Do not be afraid or terrified because of them, for the Lord your God goes with you; he *will never leave you* nor forsake you." (NIV) How cool is that? And it's true! My Immanuel is with me! He didn't forsake me. Am I any better than anyone else that I got such a quick and profound answer to prayer? Not by a long shot! And here is my encouragement to you: Get to know God. Get to know God through His word, through prayer, and through fellowship in the Spirit. You can't trust who you don't know. You can't be with somebody and not know them. This is the fellowship that God wants with us—to believe Him. To believe in the name of Jesus and to know His name. John 6:29 declares: "This is the only *work God* wants from you: Believe in the one he has sent." (NLT)

I'm no better than anyone else. And God certainly isn't playing favorites with me. I just choose to believe God. I sought His Presence and His love for me. When the Bible says that God won't let His word return to Him without accomplishing what He sent it to do, I have to believe that is exactly what God means (Isa. 55:11, NIV). Our faith has to be in the truth of God, in the knowledge of God, and in our fellowship with God. The inked words in whichever Bible you're reading don't have any power. That print won't move a mountain or bring a miracle any closer. It is knowing that God keeps His word, that He wants to be with the one who wants fellowship with Him, and that He loves us that much! Yes! God loves you that much! He will perform all His word for you.

TWO

Stepping out in Faith

Different situations demand different faiths. When I get up in the morning, I believe I'm going to continue throughout the rest of the day. When I get up in the morning and believe I'll win the lottery, that's a different kind of faith. Wouldn't that be a miracle? I don't even play the lottery! So I saw how different and flexible my faith had to be while I was on the trail.

Stepping out into faith, perhaps, could be the first kind of faith you train your spirit for if you're not strong in faith yet. You can't hike the trail until you take the first step. If you can't comprehend the faith needed for some petition or supplication, take a smaller step toward the goal—bite off what you *can* chew. Just take a step toward your God who loves you.

How do you plan four months in advance for a six-month hike? How do you plan for every day's meals, for every day's possible weather changes, for where you're going to pick up the next resupply, and whether you're going to have enough food or too much left over by the next resupply? Where do you start? Good old blogs and online guides! One might safely say, "If it's not on the internet, it doesn't exist!" All the planning guides I needed were on the internet. I just had to start looking, sift through them, and believe they were reliable.

But stepping out into faith if you're not prepared is the same thing as just showing up on the trail and expecting to make it all the way without at least planning how far you'll hike the first day. You'll probably quit after the first 15 miles. I researched, trained, and planned for four months, only to plan as far as the first 300 miles. I couldn't grasp the enormity of 2,660 miles. So I figured by the time I got to mile 300 (just an arbitrary number), I'd know what to do. And that's how it was. I learned what to do and continued. *Deuteronomy 7:22* states: "The Lord your God will drive out those nations before you, little by little. You will not be allowed to eliminate them all at once, or the wild animals will multiply around you."(NIV)

STEPPING OUT IN FAITH

The Lord God loves us so much. He won't let us bite off more than we can chew. He gives us all we need for every day—His faithfulness. My faith in what I did know and experienced helped me get through those first 300 miles. My faith in what I know about God helps me get to the next level of faith, which I need to continue in my fellowship with Him and trust in God.

I'm rather critical of Hollywood's endeavors to portray Christianity, both well and in mockery. But I have to complement their portrayal of faith in the scene in which Indiana Jones must cross a great chasm by stepping out with faith, blindly believing his foot will land on something. In *The Last Crusade*, his faith is tested to retrieve the Holy Grail to save his father. And that scene pans back and swivels to the perspective of all the hidden steps he must follow. So he steps out, makes it across, and throws sand across the steps after he's crossed to identify them for the way back. Still, he had to step out! He had to commit all that he had to that first step. His perspective of the path he had to follow was changed after he stepped out, and he was able to see beyond his faith, beyond that first step. And so it is with our trust and belief that God won't let us fail in that truly faithful moment when our hearts are focused on God's trustworthiness and abundant love for us. That is our first step to stronger and more productive faith, when we see beyond that first step of faith. God loves you that much! He will take care of you and plant your foot on that solid ground of His perfect love for you, enabling you to continue toward a more confident fellowship with Him.

I got this crazy idea to do something because I just didn't want to spend another summer in Phoenix, Arizona. I needed six months away from town to escape the brutal heat. I called my brother and threw out the suggestion of the possibility, of maybe, hiking the PCT, because it takes six months to hike. It was like putting a steak in front of dog! I don't know if thirty seconds went by before he totally set that plan in cement! "OK. When do we start?" I didn't even get the chance to suggest mountain biking the Continental Divide Trail, which was *my* first choice.

I'd never hiked anything longer than 40

miles. I didn't know how to even start to plan. My brother completed the John Muir Trail a couple of years earlier in its 220-mile entirety, and I had that going for me, in terms of starting to plan, anyway. I trust his experience. Still, it was overwhelming. I got really excited for about a week just dreaming about the whole idea, and then I came to a screeching stop. "Wait! Have you even sought God or asked Him or invited Him for this big plan of *yours*? How are you expecting to pull this off in the natural, without His guidance?"

I had to step back in order to take the first step forward. My first step needed to be to seek what God wants. Not my own imagination or ability or opportunity. Those were the things I could work with if I were so inclined. I had all three! What I needed was fellowship with God and the desire for His presence with me while I was on the trail, if that really was in His perfect plan and love for me. God gives us our hearts' desires (Ps. 37:4). God saw that He could put that desire in my heart and knew that I would respond by taking it to Him in prayer and faith, asking for His approval and presence. I really started to realize then how much God loves me. I had never experienced anything of this scale. This was a huge step in faith that I didn't know how to navigate. "You really want to do this for me?" And He loves you just as much! God loves you!

Now I could start to take the first steps to plan. I learned right there, along with my brother's advice, "You just gotta do it." You just have to start somewhere. Start! Take a step! Go! Get going! Quit moaning, and go!

Living in the reality of your faith really gets you motivated to take another step in faith to the next level (Rom. 1:17). It's exciting, invigorating, and refreshing. Yeah, I just got to see God work in that awesome way. I asked. He answered. I received. "*Ask, and ye shall receive, that your joy may be full*" (John 16:24 NKJV). My step toward what God wanted—asking for His presence, His blessing, and His guidance—was my first step in faith for this enormous endeavor. Take a step in faith. Put what you believe about God in front of you by looking at all He's done for you in the past.

THREE

Zero Day? So Soon?

When you take a day off from hiking by spending the day in one of the towns along the way to pick up a package at the post office, do laundry, or whatever else, it's referred to as a "zero day." You don't add miles to the hike away from the trail. Your mileage calculation is paused, and you add zero to your trail mileage. You've gotten this far into this book, take a zero day.

This really is supposed to be encouraging to you. God loves you so much! Maybe you're reading this and thinking to yourself that this happened to me because I'm where I am in my faith, and that's not where you are. Believe me! It takes a while, and it is a continuous walk.

I'm just a carpenter. I have no formal religious training or education. I'm not a pastor or teacher or author or leader. I just occasionally attend church, and I read my Bible every morning and pray a lot. So how can it be that I feel led by God to write what I know about my faith and share it with you so you will be encouraged? Even this is a step in faith. I know I don't want to mislead anyone into a false doctrine by writing some extrabiblical, self-help, waste-of-time bunch of worthless pages. I know I have no experience writing anything that's been published. I know I don't want my ideals to be in front of God's perfect word. I just accept that my God has given me a measure of peace in my faith through confidence in His word and made known His love to me to share with you. Because He loves you so much!

In times past, I have stumbled rigorously in my faith in God's promises to perform His word. I've prayed for people's health, for their peace and comfort, and for the strength to endure their trials. I've laid hands on friends, family, coworkers, and strangers for various requests and supplications. I believe God raises the dead back to life! And all of these I've prayed in the name of Jesus for many years! With very few signs of accomplishment, I will not retreat from believing that God performs His word! He is

God! He does the accomplishing! I will do what God has written for all of us to do and accept that my obedience will be all that God wants from me. Isaiah 49:25 states: "I will contend with him who contends with you and I will save your children."(NKJV) Wow! It's not my job to save my kids. It's my job to pray for them and be a witness for Jesus to them. That's it!

My entry-level faith was planted and sown in tithing. My folks taught me to tithe while I was young, and I haven't stopped. From Malachi 3:10, God begs us to test Him. "Hey! Check this out! Give me ten percent of you first, and you won't have enough room for what I'll give back!" I've paraphrased it a bit, but God's word is true! I've learned a lot and seen a lot from the perspective of how God has worked in my life. I'm not disappointed that I didn't see immediate answers to my prayers for others. I have to remember that God hears every prayer, and He does the impossible. I've learned from experience—God is faithful.

Hebrews 11:6 declares: "But without faith, it is impossible to please Him, for he who comes to God must believe that He is, and that He is a rewarder of those who diligently seek Him."(NKJV) Be encouraged to know that God will reward you. And back just a bit in scripture, Hebrews 10:35, 36 lets us know, "So do not throw away this confident trust in the Lord. Remember the great reward it brings you! Patient endurance is what you need now, so that you will continue to do God's will. Then you will receive all that he has promised."(NLT)

So, just like some radio hosts reply, "Hope that helps." But much more than that, it is my heart's desire for God to reveal His love for you and for His peace to cover you in His perfect grace for you, so that on this zero day, you will be encouraged to walk in a stronger faith in God. In God's love for you, I am confident!

FOUR

Having Your Own Faith

There are two mantras on the trail. Number one: you have to hike your own hike. Number two: no whining! Maybe that's why I didn't finish the trail? I hiked the PCT because my brother chose that instead of mountain biking the Great Divide Trail. I hiked the PCT because I wanted to prove I could. I hiked the PCT because all the other hikers on the trail were hiking on the trail. I hiked the PCT to avoid another Phoenix summer. I really didn't want to spend another summer in Arizona! I realized I had no other real goal or desire for completing a thru-hike. A gargantuan part of my PCT experience was not for myself. It was a mirror to me. "How do I look? Am I a PCT'er?" My faith can't rest in what you believe or how my pastor believes. That's his faith. Although I learn from his teaching about faith, I can't rely on how *he* believes. Faithfully believing, I have to plant and nurture the desire to have fellowship with my God who loves me, because my Immanuel is with me. He is with you, yearning for the same fellowship, and that's your own faith—fellowship with your loving God and Savior, knowing who you believe!

I have to have my own faith, and you have to have your own faith. All our faith needs to be in Jesus. He gave us His name to take before God in His presence to ask so our joy would be full. That's our common faith. Our personal faith, our own faith, develops in our desire to be closer to God; to want more of Him, "to know Him better, and to have the eyes of our understanding be enlightened so we may know the hope of His calling and the exceeding greatness of His power in Jesus Christ" (Eph. 1:17–19 paraphrased).

My foundation of faith is built on what I've read in the Bible—by accepting and acknowledging the grace that God has given me in my endeavors. I asked God for favor on the trail, and I received it. God allowed me favor for the entirety of the 2,660-mile-long Pacific Crest Trail. It was my fault I didn't finish. I lost my focus, my personal direction, and my own faith

HAVING YOUR OWN FAITH 21

by looking at others' experiences. I looked away from God's love for me. I had the steps. I had the favor. In deception, I chose to look elsewhere. God is still loving you! "Look to yourselves, that we do not lose those things we worked for, but that we may receive a full reward." 2 John 1:8.(KJV)

In all the favor I had and knew I had, I still found ways to complain and whine. I did a lot of whining. "Why can't I ride my mountain bike here? It's perfect for mountain biking! I *hate* switchbacks! Why is this stupid trail going there instead of straight across? I *really hate* switchbacks! Why aren't there more trail markers in snow-prone sections? *I really hate switchbacks!*"

There is no whining on the trail! Everyone there has the same bad days, the same problems, the same struggles. Why am I here in the first place? Oh yeah. I wanted to be away from Phoenix for six months. For what am I believing God in the first place?

My spirit received a spark of rejuvenation. I was reminded to seek God's kingdom and His righteousness first, and all these things will be added unto you (Matt. 6:33). God knew I needed all that stuff. I failed to accept it from Him. I forgot it was my faith in God's love for me that got me there, and as far as I got on the trail, because that was what God had provided for me. I forgot I believed, and I forgot about what God had just accomplished in me. I was able to pray with a few people along the trail—for their healing, for their futures, for their peace.

Twice, hiking partners I was with needed healing in their feet and I prayed with them. A young Caltrans workers gave my brother and me a ride to the trailhead from one of the towns. On his way to an interview for a better position, he drove out of his way to help us. I learned he needed better pay for his family and when he dropped us off I prayed with him as well. I didn't lose sight of what I had to do for others. I just got distracted by the enemy and lost my direction to my destination.

So how am I trying to encourage you with my failure? I'm one of God's children, just like you, and He wants His children to know He still loves them! God's faithfulness didn't fail. It can't fail! God is faithful! "If we are faithless, He remains faithful; He cannot deny Himself"

(2 Tim. 2:13 NKJV). I'm just as regular as the next guy. I'm going through my life, just like you. "The sin which so easily besets us," hinders me too (Heb. 12:1).

I actually had good days on the trail. On a lot of days, I really enjoyed the whole experience of hiking on a long trail. It is a beautiful trail. I took a lot of pictures. Even in the burnt areas, the topography is pronounced and cleared so one can see the hillsides and horizons without the trees. The camaraderie is fun. All those hikers from around the world and the United States, everyone expecting something different, but with one experience in common. I was blessed, and you are blessed as well. God loves you that much, and He wants you to have enough of your own faith in His love for you.

FIVE

Navigational Faith

Throughout Southern California, the Pacific Crest Trail is marked pretty well, and the trail is easy to follow when it's not under snow. Although a number of other hikers in a stretched-out group I was with had a really difficult time navigating to the summit of Mount Baden-Powell because of the snow, we made it and continued. But I also lost the trail several other times and spent a few extra hours bushwhacking my way back. A few of those times were because *I hate switchbacks*. Others were the result of seeing on a map that it's shorter if I just go over the hill instead of around it, only to find out later, after exhausting effort both up the hill and down, that I misread the map in haste and missed my connection back to the trail. Halfmile Maps offers a three-hundred-page set of really good maps for the PCT, and they are absolutely useful! Thank you, Halfmile

Maps! I relied on those maps even if I read them incorrectly!

My faith is the same way. I can follow God's word and the examples of others from the Bible, and I'll be OK and be able to stay on the right path. When I want something now, or sooner than later, I misread God's word and look for a shortcut, only to get way off the right path.

Throughout the Old Testament, God urges and prompts us to "Look up!" Look up from where you are. Look up to where you're going. Luke 21:28 encourages us to "Look up. For our redemption draweth nigh." I noticed that when we look down at the path continuously, we focus on what's immediately in front of us, eventually losing the trail or missing out on some wonder because we failed to look up. It's natural to look down when you're backpacking. The weight of the pack bends you over. You don't want to trip and/or fall. It's what you do—you watch where you go. But you gotta look up sometime. I know three of the hikers with whom I periodically hiked missed a beautiful and awesome milestone landmark, missed a trail-junction marker, and wandered about for three hours. The third actually hiked in the opposite direction for three extra miles to add six miles to that day. That's a lot of extra miles added to one's daily mileage.

They got so wrapped up in going, so dedicated in going the distance, so performance driven, they missed out on the gracious beauty of Eagle Rock, lost a half day of hiking time, and just plain went backward. All of them looking down at the trail. The section of the Sierras I went through was so covered in snow that traveling over the mountain passes and through the valleys was fast because there were no switchbacks, and we just went straight through the valleys. We traveled so fast that I missed a lot of famous rock formations, ones that I really wanted to see up close. I forgot to look up, having attained a gentle trot on snowshoes and wanting to get to that next campsite.

I've navigated my faith that way a few times too. I was so dedicated to doing this certain way of praying or believing in that certain way of expectation ("Line upon line. Precept upon precept." Isa. 28:13). I was the one who couldn't make God's faithfulness work. In my zealotry, I took away God's ability to answer. But I also observed attention to detail on the map, pointing out the way for a group I was with. I looked up and saw where we needed to go. Going forward and desiring the end result is as necessary as looking up to our Father in heaven, who is the one who performs and accomplishes our petitions and supplications and guides us in our faith. Looking up to the Lord God should be our first faithful navigational tool upon which we perpetually rely.

GPS is great as long as the batteries last. Solar chargers and battery packs have totally enhanced a hiker's experience and peacefully settled a backpack full of anxiety. Maps and compasses are still staples of the "ten essentials," but technology is terrific! I only learned how to make the technology work for me a week before I quit the trail, and then I didn't have enough battery life! I had the tech all along; I just didn't know if I was using it right. I either followed my brother when I was with him, followed other hikers when I was with them, or went along with my intuition and guessed what my GPS unit had said when I hiked by myself. My own faith was set aside to ride along in the convenience of others' abilities in their own faith of their technology and knowledge of how to use it.

A compass is handy, especially if you're going in the opposite direction (poor Hobo Max, he's the one who went backward for three miles). On some parts of the trail, when snow covers the trail through a couple mountain passes and north is obscured by confusing lighting, a compass is handy. But if you start at the Mexican border and head north, or at least follow the signs, you should be able to make it. Your goal is north! What we know from the Bible is that God is faithful, and He loves us that much to orient us so that our goal and our direction is toward Him. God's Positioning System, *GPS*, generally speaking, is if we believe in the Bible, we ought to know where our destination is. If we want all that God's trail has for us, turn by turn, step by step, our *GPS* needs to be charged up in the knowledge of who God is and what He wants to do for us. *GPS* is communication with the Divine Source that is always around us: God and His Holy Spirit.

GPS tells me where I am. All the apps and data used in a handheld navigational device tell me what's around me. With *GPS*, if I listen, God tells me where I am. His Holy Spirit is His app and data that show me everything around me. "A Lamp unto our feet and a Light unto our path" (Ps. 119:105 KJV). I am surrounded by God's Holy Spirit continually updating and refreshing my spirit, my spiritual location in relationship to His presence—the signal I *need* to be using – His *GPS*. Orientation toward God's fellowship and presence becomes following in His steps, seeking His paths, and believing His direction. He loves us so much. He'll hold our hands and pick us up to carry us if we are weary (Isa. 46:3–4). He wants to be our Immanuel—God with us.

When I realize God is true and faithful, and His word is true and faithful, I'm using my navigational tools in my faith to get closer to my God who loves me—His will for my destination. I had to learn how to use all that technology, and I didn't learn well, because I like shortcuts. God gave us His Holy Spirit to teach us in all things (John 14:26). When we use God's word through His Holy Spirit, we already know how to use His word. Find God's direction for you with the tools that He has provided, teaching us how to use then properly. Seeing where that compass of God's true word is pointing saves a lot of wasted time, and you get to see the wonders along the way. Establish that *GPS* exchange of communication—your prayers and desire for God, His direction and love for you. He knows what we need before we ask (Matt. 6:8 and Isa. 65:24). His signal is always available and pointing toward us. He loves you that much!

SIX

False Faith

God is not a genie in a bottle! God is not the genie from the magic lamp! God's word isn't a compilation of incantations constantly repeated to conjure up everything we want! Warning: not using God's product as directed will result in harm!

I can't just start wanting something and expect to receive it because I want it or ask for it. The Believe It/Receive It and Name It/Claim It movement had some true biblically based principles that needed to be followed. The enemy and deceiver lied to us and made us look for an easier way, replacing those true principles with the fleshly excitement of receiving whatever we wanted—shortcuts to how God directs our paths. God's love for you requires your fellowship with Him to follow His designated path.

But oh boy, do I like shortcuts! I wholly believe there are legitimate shortcuts. Some truly save time, money, effort, and stress. Somehow I can't justify hiking twenty miles of trail when I can actually physically see the trail beside the road and only hike twelve road miles. The road is straight, but the trail winds in and out and up and down so many hills. Road hiking is harder on your feet, but eight miles less allows for plenty of comfortable recovery time. A husband and wife who were on the trail with me at different times were purists, and that's a good thing. They *had* to hike every step on the trail, and that's a good thing. They completed the trail, and I didn't. It's still a good thing. I can see where my failure lies because the trail became burdensome to me. It became advancements in meaninglessness, looking at rocks and hauling water. Because it wasn't my own hike, I had to find shortcuts to make it go by faster.

I tried to avoid a long section of contouring switchbacks (a really long section) just before Tehachapi, California. It became a race between me and a younger, faster group I was with for a few days. We just got rain, hail, and snow the night before. From where we camped, it was just over twenty-two miles to reach the road and hitchhike to town and zero. Wet, tired, and too proud to be left behind, twice, I saw I could take a shortcut and beat them.

The first shortcut, I went up the wrong ridge and ended up behind that group (humiliated), but I cut the switchbacks there and went straight down the mountain and passed them (happily proud). The second shortcut, I saw a straight road on the map that paralleled the trail. It was in the valley below a series of other ridges—the contouring switchbacks—ahead of us. The map made it look like a legitimate county dirt road. The group caught up to me and passed me (humiliated again). They got so far ahead of me that they were almost finished with their break by the time I caught up to them. This second shortcut was right around the corner and out of sight from their break location. If I ran down the mountain fast enough, I thought they wouldn't see me trying to cheat the trail.

I got to the road in impressive form. Nice road too! There were even No Trespassing signs facing the road. I hadn't passed any on the way down, so I kind of had a legitimate excuse. "Hey, there weren't any signs up there," I smugly thought to myself as a weak excuse. I stayed on the road because of the signs. Solitarily hiking in the pride of my primacy and almost to the main road, a guy came along in a truck coming up the road as I was heading down. He pulled over and asked what I was doing on private property and how I had gotten there. Before I could answer, he started to vehemently declare that all that land and the road was private property, and it was hikers like me who ruin it for everyone else to the point that property owners want to close access to the trail because it crosses their land. He went on to say that he had to escort me to the main road and call the sheriff. "Get in the truck! I don't have time to wait for you to hike to the road!" He made sure I saw he had a revolver on the seat next to him. Fearfully polite and entirely apologetic for my rebellious reroute, and on behalf of the other hikers on the PCT, I honestly accepted the consequences of my pride. I didn't even begin to excuse myself. I was wrong. I didn't show him the map that made the road look useable. I didn't say, "Hey, there weren't any signs up there." I was wrong. He asked me if I wanted him to call the sheriff, and I told him that was up to him; that was his right and his property. Through God's grace and some honesty on my part, I was released from my violation. We parted on amicable and well-wished terms, and my arrival on the main road became bitterly humbling.

God showed me favor, but I soured and putrefied a public relationship, which has real consequences. Stay on the trail. My false faith in my physical ability to handle some gnarly terrain didn't bring glory to God. The parents at the principal's office aren't throwing a party after they bring their child home. My false faith expected God to work in my favor to get me to the main road first. "Pride goes before a fall" (Prov. 16:18).

The reason I can share this encouragingly is that even when we're wrong, way wrong, God always loves us. Say it out loud: "God loves me that much!" The parents leaving the principal's office in a number of emotions still love their child. God loves you that much! God's love never fails! God is Love!

Your own faith and false faith can disastrously be the same thing. The class of 2017 PCT finishers, I believe, all had love for the trail. It became what sustained them from border to border. I have enormous respect for the forces of nature and my surroundings. I consider myself an experienced and qualified mountaineer. Having scaled mountains and huge expanses of rock formations in all four seasons and having been a well-trained volunteer backcountry search-and-rescue personnel responder, I have my own faith, physically speaking, in my abilities and I learned respect in what I had experienced. I loved all the trails I was blessed to have completed. I failed to love the Pacific Crest Trail through not hiking my own hike, whining and wanting to complete it *my* way. I had the ability. I had the opportunity. I had my own faith in myself, and it proved false. I didn't love what would have brought me success; that is, like everyone else, everything I was going through on the trail. I believe we have to love all the adversity we seem to see in our struggles in faith (Hab. 3:17–19).

I can say, "I love God." Is my love for God what sustains me in my pilgrimage to Him? I can respect Him because I have faith that His word is true, and like forces of nature, I will get knocked down if I don't respect Him. How can I identify the love I need to reach the goal? To receive my petitions? Walking closer to our God, who loves us and sustains us and rewards

FALSE FAITH

us, puts us closer to Him. Our Immanuel is with us. Faith in the trail that gets you from Mexico to Canada and embracing it with your life affords you success. Faith in God who loves you and gets you from confusion to peace (Jer. 29:4), embracing His presence and love, even when you can't possibly begin to understand the bigger picture, that's the love that God effectively uses (Philem. 1:5–6). Look up!

SEVEN

Nero Day ... Not a Full Zero
(Hey, Just Sharin' What They Say on the Trail)

I'm learning as I'm writing. Sitting in front of my computer, diligently dishing out my take of the PCT experience, I'm still not seeing God's bigger picture. I feel I am forcefully sequestered to my home until I've written the last word. My cable modem went out, so I have no internet. I have no TV service. I've been nursing an injured ankle for four weeks. I'm not even working on stuff for my business—I'm nowhere near retirement age, so I still have to work. My distraction excuses have been sequestered! Being "compelled to write" would seem like a vacation. At least I could lessen the degree to which I must accomplish this adventure. Listening to my pastor's exciting messages on Sundays is putting gas on the fire, but as a shout-out to my girls and their enjoyment of the Spice Girls, I'm still asking God, "So tell me what You want, what You really, really want." And God's reply remains, "I'll tell you what to write, what to really, really write. Keep writing!" At least I don't have to lie on one side for a year (Ezek. 4:4) or walk around naked for another three years (Isa. 20:3). I can only describe a true peace I feel when I believe that God will encourage you to trust Him by pressing on.

EIGHT

Sharing Faith

More accurately, my faith and trust in Jesus as God who loves me is nurtured and established enough to share the good times and faithful answers with people. The actual sharing as witnessing, or positioning myself to receive a petition from God kind of faith, is yet another step. I mentioned earlier that the Pacific Crest Trail is beautiful. That could be an understatement to some. From beginning to end there is such admirable, stunning beauty at every step. Springtime flowers and grasses. Budding trees and hues of light in the sky. Snowcapped peaks and snow-covered basins if you're lucky enough to be hiking in a good snow year. There are really beautiful snakes along the trail that represent the loving variety of God's imagination. Insects and wildlife alike adorn the hillsides. Edible plants and berries along the way to eat as you walk. My regular diet on the trail was sustained by the enormous abundance of wild onions and miner's lettuce. Just grab and keep going! Rock formations that seem to dwarf high-rise buildings. Ledges so high above deep canyons that the walls are vertical and so close to the trail that actual precaution and reverence are required for the safety of one's life. Vistas going on for miles—beyond a hundred miles on good days, depending on where one is. It's beautiful, and I can tell you about it because I was there. This is sharing faith. I lived it enough to share it with you. I've lived my own faith in God enough to share His faithfulness with you.

I also mentioned I took a lot of pictures, 792 to be exact, and that wasn't even halfway. Happy selfies, sad selfies, selfies with friends and with the locals. Pictures of trail magic containers, which are ice chests or metal containers filled with snacks, food, and drinks that volunteers place along the trail just for hikers. Yeah, some people are kind enough and considerate enough to help you along the way. It's all there for you. Just don't be greedy. Pictures of all that beauty, which refreshes and changes throughout each day. Pictures of favorite campsites. Pictures

SHARING FAITH

of the campsites that were miserable to be in because of temporary conditions.

By now there has to be some evidence of progress. Is there a shoot of faith popping out of the ground yet? Has any faith in God blessed you with a fond recollection of "that time when ..." All of God's entire word is given to us to remind us of all His perfect love for us. It is beautiful along the way. "His mercies are new every morning" (Lam. 3:22, 23). We take pictures along the way to remind us where we've been, the emotions we've had, and the moments in our lives that affected our souls, additionally to prove to someone, "Hey, I'm not just making this up!" Those pictures of God's love exposed in the basins of our hearts spur us on to continue with Him and move closer toward Him—they develop into those images we hang on our walls with cherished memories that remind us of what had happened. It will happen again as our fellowship with Immanuel continues to grow.

Right next to the pictures of our kids and relatives are pictures of good times, friends, and accomplishments. God has the same picture book in heaven, filled with pictures of you in your great moments of faith and trust in Him (Mal. 3:16). God is pointing to His pictures of you, wanting to tell you, "That's you when you were little. That's when you told that person I loved them. Here's when you asked for My help. And here's you when you got My help." God just loves you so much. He reminds himself in that book of remembrance just how proud He is of you and your trust in Him. "That's My child! Oh how I love 'em!" Wow! That's powerful! That's God's powerful love for you.

I could stop now on such a plateau as that! But I don't know if there's a section in bookstores called really short stories. Besides, God still has encouragement for you that I need to share.

NINE

Perfect Vision Faith

Some of us need glasses. I'm still in denial, but I use reading glasses. Not everybody completes all 2,660 miles of the Pacific Crest Trail. The PCTA, the managing organization of the PCT, estimated thirty-five hundred applicants for 2016 and up to fifteen hundred more for 2017. I'm taking a shortcut to fact-checking. Because of California's huge snowfall in 2017, a much larger percentage of those who started the hike failed. If 40 percent of the hikers who planned on hiking the entire PCT in 2017 failed because of the profuse amount of snow, that's two thousand hikers who didn't make it. I'm one of them. That's a moderate estimate when a 20 percent success rate is considered good!

My vision of success waned in my straining attempts to shortcut, in my repeated and extended zero days, in skipping over such a huge section of snow-covered trail in the Sierras (four hundred miles) to avoid the dangerous, overflowing snowmelt-swollen rivers. I couldn't focus any longer on the end result of my attempt to complete the trail. Advancements in meaninglessness dimmed what I saw with great clarity when I started, but I had to strain to see by the time I reached my end in Northern California.

"Why continue if I can't complete the entire trail?" I asked myself. I should've asked, "Why stop when there's so much more to see?" But that's just it. I became visionless and blind to the overwhelming beauty of Oregon and Washington. I felt I would've had to grope around in the darkness of my failure for not entirely completing the 2,660-mile trail. I had imperfect vision. I failed to see the bigger image of the beauty of the Pacific Crest Trail through everywhere it leads.

There's no way a movie can convey the effects of everything one encounters on the trail. Books and stories, even this allegory, can't begin to portray or explain it. You have to see it for yourself! Then, after having perfectly understood what someone else was trying to share, your vision of the trail is enlightened. For some, that enlightenment lasts to the border terminus

PERFECT VISION FAITH

and beyond. For others, myself included, it is a momentary flash of inspiration. The same way a flash of lightning at night illuminates an entire landscape, but afterwards, the direction is lost in darkness.

The Lord God who loves you sees you in perfection. If God uses glasses, they are the atoning blood of Jesus, His sacrifice on the cross, and His resurrection from the dead. We can't be seen by God any other way. God can't look at sin (Hab. 1:13). He has to see me—He has to see you—in perfection through Jesus! "We are to be perfect, just as our Heavenly Father is perfect" (Matt. 5:48 paraphrased NKJV). "The Lord will perfect that which concerns me" (Ps. 138:8 NKJV). God also completes what He starts (Phil. 1:6) and makes us complete (Col. 2:10). God finishes His trail because He sees perfectly!

The eyes of perfection gaze into our eyes, a veil having been removed, to lift the scales of blindness from our perceptions of where we are. Look up into the eyes of Jesus! God so loves you. He sees you in His perfection. He sees you where you can't see yourself. He is eternal and beyond our dimension of time and location. He is with us continually to ensure His success in what He began. God wipes away the lies of the enemy, who blinds us with the deceit of accusation and guilt and the shortcut distractions of falsely dutiful repetitious works that, when we're tired of laboring, just make us sink in the mire of disillusionment.

God, Immanuel, loves you so much! His perfect vision embraces our end, and it is with Him in glory. By focusing on our perfect destination, the completion of our quest is our corrected vision to follow the true direction of fellowship with God. Look up!

TEN

Nutritional Faith

Oh boy! And yee-haw! We get to eat! Come and get it! A deciding factor for me in not planning to hike another thru-trail or the entire PCT again is the tremendously enormous and not-for-the-faint-of-heart task of planning meals. It is a huge amount of work and effort. Breakfast and dinner each day for the entirety of the trail. Lunch for all those days, too, if that's the way you hike—and all the snacks in between! You really do go through that many calories and that much energy every day. And zero days will drain your wallet before you're halfway through because there's so much good food to buy in every town you visit. Eating all the time is as necessary as hiking all day to finish the trail, and yet weight loss becomes inevitable! It's what you do. You eat like a pig and still lose weight.

Freeze-dried food is essential for both

nutrition and saving weight in your backpack. The bummer about it is all the sodium and the portion sizes. I bought the big number ten cans of several different varieties of freeze-dried dinners and breakfasts; then I portioned them into Ziploc bags—one meal per bag. The cans listed so many portions per can, and I always ended up with three or four portions less than that number because I put more into each of the bags than directed! It ain't cheap either! On the trail those portioned meals were hardly enough. It's insane what one has to ingest while searching for more water and gadding about to the next campsite! Oh, there's that whining again!

Hey, as long as I'm already negative about this—water! Water, especially in drought years (fortunately, 2017 was a plentiful and cooler year than previous ones), is always the premium and predominant taskmaster of the hike. It is at the top of the list of everything you *have* to have. You need to hydrate. There were some sections where we (the hikers within a day or two of me, in front and behind) had to carry five to six liters of water a day through the deserts and dry sections, sometimes carrying six to eight liters for a couple of days in a row. That's roughly

NUTRITIONAL FAITH

seventeen pounds of water added to what we were already carrying. The amount of all the gear you need, plus some food, is equal to just a day or two of water, and then you have to look for more! I joked to myself about that to justify carrying that much weight. "I was hauling water from Mexico to Canada. When I realized the Canadians didn't need it, I quit!"

Trail angels are the volunteers who, of their own volition and monetary resources, take huge supplies of water and food to the trail and leave them there for all the hikers passing by. Thank God for human kindness. In the middle of a long, hot, and dry day, hiking up to one of those caches of water and food immediately lifts one's spirit. Water by the gallons! Candy, beer, wine, cookies, fresh fruit, soda! Oh yeah! The veritable cornucopia of salacious satisfaction rewarding you for your valiant and triumphant achievement...of just getting there! Indeed! We have our own trail angels ministering to us daily (Heb. 1:14).

While all the planning one must struggle through to be fed on the trail seems tedious, monotonous, and expensive, it all must be done! When He was *hungry*, Jesus declared, "It is written: 'Man shall not live on bread alone, but on every word that comes from the mouth of God'" (Matt. 4:4 NKJV). How do you establish the nutrition you need to keep hiking? Internet, books, magazines, and classes. They all have sample meals and nutritional statements for each meal they suggest. Eat this. Eat that. Eat more of that than this. It's all there.

Our faith needs the body-building nutrition fed to us by the mouth of God, supplemented with prayer and fellowship with our Immanuel. The demands of spiritual living and exercising our faith *must* be met by God's perfect word. As babes, we desire the milk of the word (1 Pet. 2:2). And solid food, in our experienced maturity, to discern and distinguish (Heb. 5:14).

I got cranky when I didn't eat regularly. When I work, I don't normally take a break. I just work all day, and maybe if I've packed a snack and remember that I have it, I'll eat it. That's what it was like for me on the trail too. I just didn't want to stop for a break and eat. But I used a lot more energy on the trail, and my fatigue displayed itself with louder announcement.

We will get physically cranky when we

don't fill up on God's word if we're used to it. If we're not used to satisfying our spiritual appetites with God's word, then we're always just scrounging around for a morsel of worldly garbage that won't satisfy us. From trash can to trash can, dumpster diving for leftovers from those who were satisfied. Because our spirit is joined together with God's Spirit, the Spirit of the Lord (1 Cor. 6:14), a fast of time by not regularly engaging in spiritual edification starves us, taking away the peace and blessing of fellowship with our God who loves us so much. "When your words came, I ate them; they were my joy and my heart's delight, for I bear your name, Lord God Almighty" (Jer. 15:16 NIV).

ELEVEN

Another Nero!

It takes me about a day or two to get through a chapter of writing. So a few days (chapters) ago, I was lamenting my sequestration. God is Good! He heard my heart's desire and listened. I'm an active guy. I must have playtime throughout the week—ride my bike, go hiking with a friend or my son, be outside doing something, even if it's work. Yesterday I got to go cross-country skiing in Flagstaff, Arizona. It was the day after their first snow of the season, and the skiing was absolutely fantastic! I broke first tracks in the backcountry. More than a foot and a half of snow fell, and I was the only one on the trail! Oh, that was a good day.

I was at a men's group a couple of days before. It was my first time with that group from our church, and the leader of the group asked us what our pastor's message from the previous Sunday meant to us. He first shared how looking up was how he wanted to hike instead of looking down at the trail as he does. Looking up to God, he explained, would lead us through what we fail to see, by accepting the bigger picture of what God sees.

My pastor's message a few weeks ago was about our "withness" with God, Immanuel. All this combined confirmation and agreement in the Spirit is encouraging! I also shared earlier how I was sort of doubting this writing. But after a glimpse of what the Holy Spirit is doing, how these events are unfolding, I believe I'm on the right track. I can share this, believing that this is encouraging someone, even you. God loves you that much!

TWELVE

Knowing Faith

It appears as though I have all this joy and good stuff going on, even in light of my incapacity to complete a long trail. It's not all fun and games for everyone; of that I am also confident. There are some in the world who have suffered abuse from others. Some who have had the tremendous burden of the loss of a loved one or have been the victim of heinous crimes. I was very recently reminded of the sad world we live in because of the curse of sin in the world. Reminded so much so that I was brought to tears by the news I heard on the radio. I was driving and almost had to stop to plead with God to somehow extend a measure of peace or consolation to the victims of this heinous and repulsive abuse.

It's very heavy on my heart right now, and my fervent prayers are with those victims for their deliverance from such emotional trauma, for God to cover them with His perfect love, lifting them up from the mire of the enemy's brutal attack on their lives.

Among the several people who died in swollen and fast-moving rivers in 2017, two were PCT hikers. To the community of PCT'ers, that loss was all the more significant because of the connection to the Trail. Some of us were just a day or two away from the same crossing or maybe even a couple hours away, but didn't realize that a fellow hiker had just lost their life crossing a river which was now in front of us, or one that we had just crossed. This connection should extend to all our fellow humans. We all have a dangerous crossing ahead of us somewhere.

Knowing the faith in God who loves becomes the only thing that seems important. Following this faithful trail to our perfect destination, to our loving God and Savior, is God's will for us, compelling us to seek out the true and delivering scriptures that we can use to share with those who have not seen the glorious presence of God who loves you. "Blessed be the God and Father of our Lord Jesus Christ, the Father of compassion and the God of all comfort, who comforts us in all our troubles, so that we can comfort those in any trouble with the comfort we ourselves have received from God" (2 Cor. 1:3–4 NKJV). Knowing that we all must encourage those precious in the sight of God siblings of ours—we're all God's children—should instill the most powerful motivation to earnestly pray for them. God loves us so much! "Since prayer is at the bottom of all this, what I want mostly is for men to pray—not shaking angry fists at enemies but raising *holy hands* to God" (1 Tim. 2:8 MSG).

Sharing faith needs that next step into the sharing of our faith—what we've experienced through God's gracious love and care for us. Been there? Done that? Now's a good time to put that knowledge to use. Now's a great time to be the love of God to someone who hasn't been as fortunate. Through God's Holy Spirit, lift up the chin of those victims and those who have suffered the loss of their loved ones by asking God to perform His perfect word of love to them, that they would come to know how precious they are to God who loves them.

The trail is hard sometimes, harder than we really want to deal with. The finishers dealt with the hardships and succeeded. They have the reward of knowing that they endured and kept the faith. "I have fought the good fight, I have finished the race, I have kept the faith. Henceforth there is laid up for me the crown of righteousness, which the Lord, the righteous judge, will award to me on that Day, and not only to me but also to all who have loved his appearing" (2 Tim. 4:7–8 NKJV).

I left the Sierras to avoid risking my life in dangerous river crossings. Most of the finishers skipped these areas, too, when the snow was still heavy, but they later went back to make up those missing miles. The hiking partner I left in the Sierras had the stamina and devotion to continue. In the midst of hardship, she wouldn't give in. Our paths separated with great and fond emotions because we both knew that she'd be alone to face the danger, while I'd be leaving all that for the convenience of shortcuts and easier hiking. We parted in tears for each other. I had to pause on the trail, kneeling to pray and ask God for direction. And when I chose to leave that section, I prayed for her safety and her success. With a hug and tears, we bid each other farewell.

KNOWING FAITH

I really felt bad when I left her! She was hiking with me because I had the experience and the capability to handle those conditions. She didn't have the very necessary experience, and I left her alone—a very lousy time to hike my own hike! After making it to Canada, she finished the trail by going back to hike the section she eventually had to skip for her own safety. In spite of a painful memory, I believe we've become friends with a special bond between us.

God loves you so much! He will never leave you! He will never hurt you! He sacrificed hiking His own hike for you by sending Jesus to die on the cross for you! He didn't just go His own way when our sins separated us. In His sacrifice of Jesus for us, God continued with us. That's knowing faith, which has the power to deliver, the power to heal, and the power to love like God loves! And that is God's powerful love for you. Own it! Live it! Share it!

All this goes way beyond the trail. The victims, the lonely ones, the ones who cry out in anguish, the divorced and cheated against ones, the ones without the faith that can lift them up. We who have the faith must find that verse of deliverance and pray that verse to God, asking Him to perform His healing word over those who seem to have been left alone! "And now, for a little while, grace has been shown from the Lord our God to leave us a remnant to escape and to give us a peg in His holy place, that our God may enlighten our eyes and give us a measure of revival in our bondage" (Ezra 9:8 NKJV). Break the chain of the enemy's bondage and lies. "Lord God, give them the Light on the road which they should travel" (Nehemiah 9:12b NKJV).

THIRTEEN

Expecting Faith
(What Will This Conception Grow Into?)

It was only a month and a few days after my wife passed away that this hiking plan of mine was conceived. As I had mentioned earlier, my brother jumped right in, and there it was—let's go hiking for six months! I wasn't on a mission of consolation or grief-driven escapism. I really did not want to spend another summer in Phoenix. Now, being unattached and my kids being adults, I had no real obligations or hindrances that kept me from going. This was an opportunity, not an extended mourning.

"Many are *the plans* in a person's heart, but it is the Lord's purpose that prevails" (Prov. 19:21 NKJV). With all the planning that I had to do in the physical realm, a questionable apprehension of doubt still lingered: What about the snow? What's going to happen at home while I'm gone for six months? What's going to happen along the trail? I didn't doubt that my prayers to God were heard and answered. I wholeheartedly believed I had the favor I asked for at that time. I suppose anyone with as big a plan as this gets a bit anxious. Things went as planned. I expected some things to go certain ways, and they did. My fellowship with my Immanuel was really growing, and I was confident in the direction I was going.

My expectation was to visit my parents for a week before I started the trail. While I was there, my faith in sharing what God wanted me to share was thrown at me like a curveball! "Oh yeah? Believe this, Mr. Faithful!" I was batted into a ministry for a loved one that was way out of the ballpark of tradition. This message of God's love for that person was such a radical concept in its theology that I knew it couldn't be from me. I just had to go with it. "Just do it" was all I could hear God tell me. We have a loving Savior and an all-knowing God. The message was heard and received with such a beautiful change of heart. A new child of Christ was born and wed to Him the same day—I tell you the truth! I didn't plan that!

That pointed the direction of the trail I was

EXPECTING FAITH

going to be on for the rest of the time I was on the PCT. I couldn't help but reflect on that afternoon while I hiked the trail. I was told two additional times to minister God's perfect love to someone who so needed to hear a message of love from a God who loved them so much.

My expectation was to hike. God's deliverance was for His children, that His love would be born in their spirit to grow and be fruitful. For me, this has grown into my own hike to my perfect destination: my loving Heavenly Father. I desire to have plenty of adventures, and I plan to ask my Immanuel for His approval, and I'll do so with the expectation of being used in any way God sees fit. Such is my faith in expectation. I expect God's purpose to prevail.

FOURTEEN

Faith after Disillusionment

After I left the Sierras, I had about ten days of just driving around the entire state of California with my brother. San Diego to Mount Shasta and then into Oregon, stopping in Reno for a couple of hours for a camper shell and to pick up packages that I had mailed ahead to various post offices along the trail (resupply boxes). No complaints for all that. I got to see what was ahead of me. I got to catch up on my communications, but I developed a faint lack of motivation to continue, almost like I had gotten soft during my time off.

Finally getting back onto the trail, from mile 831 in the Sierras, skipping to mile 1,262 in northern California, I was a mile in before I started to hike through snow again. I had just returned the boots I used in the Sierras to the store I bought them from because the Gore-Tex label was totally misleading. The boots were soaked just four miles into my restart at Kearsarge Pass, way back in the Sierras. So I was back in my regular ineffective-in-snow boots. I didn't pack my crampons or ice ax, because I didn't think I'd need them. With more attempts to short-cut the trail, I stumbled around in the signless snow (no trail markers), trying to map read and navigate with GPS while draining the batteries of the two solar chargers I had and the GPS unit I was using. I finally knew how to use the trail app that I downloaded onto my phone, but the phone battery was dying too!

Frustrated to the uttermost, I decided to just follow a ridge in the general direction I needed to go and ignore trying to find the actual trail. It's not that bad of a concept; it worked in the Sierras. The trail moved west at the end of the ridge, and I had to change course. By the time I had gotten to the turning point, I realized I had to really bushwhack to get back to the general direction or backtrack quite a ways to get there.

Always forward! Jumping into mountain shrubbery, with a heavy pack, seemed doable at the time. It's not called bushwhacking for nothing. I got a few steps over the branches before I slipped and flipped upside down, rolling into the midst of the shrubs. Somewhat stuck, with a heavy pack tangled in the branches, I worked my way out and did a gear check at the bottom of the hill, hoping I didn't break or lose anything. I shook it off and continued. Only about twenty minutes away from there, I reached for my maps to verify my direction, and I discovered that I had lost all my maps. My head dropped in despair.

Go back? I don't even know where I lost them! Maybe in the shrubs, but that was on a hill, and going uphill through all that was next to impossible. The mosquitoes were starting to get significantly annoying. I just lost 150 miles worth of maps, and my tech gear was failing. There were no trail signs. There was no trail to be seen or followed in the snow, and ... *forget this*! I'm done! It's not worth it!

It was only a twenty-mile stretch from where I started to the town ahead. But with the struggle to navigate and the lousy footing I had with the wrong boots for the snow, it took me two days to get there. I had to hitchhike to another town about seventy-five miles ahead to pick up a new backpack that I had sent to the post office there, which gave me a lot of time to brood about the entire dilemma. What a letdown. What a waste of money. But more than all that, I felt deep down inside that I had let God down. I had healing, favor, blessing. Sure, there were the regular bad times before, but God got me through them (Neh. 9:18–21).

> [18] Even after they had cast an image of a calf for themselves and said, "This is your God who brought you out of Egypt," and they had committed terrible blasphemies,
> [19] You did not abandon them in the wilderness because of Your great compassion. During the day the pillar of cloud never turned away from them, guiding them on their journey. And during the night the pillar of fire illuminated the way they should go.
> [20] You sent Your good Spirit to instruct them. You did not withhold Your manna from their mouths, and You gave them water for their thirst.
> [21] You provided for them in the wilderness 40 years and they lacked nothing. Their clothes did not wear out, and their feet did not swell.
>
> *Holman Christian Standard Bible* (HCSB)

I really wanted to get a thousand miles hiked before I quit. I only needed two hundred more miles! Compared to eight hundred, two hundred seemed easy. But I just lost my maps! I lost all that time driving around. I had to wait another day for the new pack. And although I didn't know for two more weeks, I had lost my water filter as well. These excuses didn't add up to the faith I was reveling in. I was enabled to enjoy an experience of a lifetime, but all I did was pity myself into disillusionment. How could I be so insecure in my faith as to let God down like that? I know there's a scripture for this somewhere in the Bible. Perhaps you'll find it for me.

It was the latter part of June when I quit. Since I left all my nontrail stuff at my folk's place before I started the hike, I went back there for a couple days and finished up goodbyes before I went back to Phoenix. The middle of June? That's the beginning of summer! Didn't I want to be away for the summer? On the way back home, about sixty miles from town, the digital thermometer in the car was reading 119 degrees! I took a picture of it so I could say I wasn't making it up. OK, I guess I had that coming.

I lost my focus on my true faith and decided to try and avoid the hard test of my faith by quitting. But God still loves us when we quit! He still loves us when we don't want to test our faith. God is Love! *"For whom the Lord loves He reproves, even as a father corrects the son in whom he delights"* (Prov. 3:12 NKJV).

I let go of God's guiding hand. I jumped out of His loving arms, wanting my own way. That changed the outcome of my hike, but that didn't change God's love for me. Whatever step back or away from your faith you may have taken, don't let that become a stumbling block to your fellowship with God who loves you. Immanuel won't leave you—He is with you. Look up into the perfect eyes of Jesus and accept His love for you. God loves you that much!

FIFTEEN

Shaking-the-Crud-off Faith

The enemy is such a liar! Even as he is the father of lies, he's one smart liar! Guilt or wanting to hold on to the bad we've done—a lying way to own up to our offenses—is entirely from the devil! The sacrifice of Jesus did away with all the accusations, judgments, and guilt, all of which we should set down at the foot of the cross. That's the whole point of Jesus's sacrifice in the first place—to free us from our bondage to those lies from Satan and to make us perfect in the eyes of God.

I enjoyed a significant portion of my time on the Pacific Crest Trail. You've read the majority of how I squandered and trifled such a great blessing. Encouragement now becomes the only real topic I can address with any aptitude of measure. I can faithfully exclaim that God loves you so much! He is always near you and with you to pick you up and carry you along the way. While this may seem distant to some who still want to hold on to the bad in their lives because the enemy has such a great false excuse, the matter of standing on the true word of God, believing He hears, He answers, He loves, and He always provides now takes preeminence over all the crud we think is hindering our progress. No doubt, life is a tough row to hoe, and a trail of reoccurring and sometimes monumental hardships and setbacks can't be avoided. Nevertheless, God loves you. He is wanting and waiting to help us and show us the right direction. He is faithful to perform His word in our lives to light the way in which we should travel *(Ps. 119:130 Bible Study Tools)*. "Break open your words. Let the light shine out; let ordinary people see the meaning. No sooner do they gain admission into the soul than they enlighten it." Our joy, which God provides, and our desires, which He wants to accomplish, let us see the wonders along the way, looking up to Him, who faithfully navigates our course toward a real and prosperous fellowship with Him.

We get to enjoy God's proximity in whatever endeavor we step out in, believing through fellowship with Him that the foundation of our faith is the tested gear worthy of the challenge we will put it through. "But solid food is for the mature, who by constant use have trained themselves to distinguish good from evil" (Heb. 5:14 NKJV). The constant use of our fellowship trains us to know how to use our spiritual gear and how to get the best use out of it. "Finally, be strong in the Lord and in his mighty power. Put on the full armor of God, so that you can take your stand against the devil's schemes" (Eph. 6:10 NIV).

SIXTEEN

Winding It Up

James 1:12 states: "*Blessed is the man who remains steadfast under trial, for when he has stood the test he will receive the crown of life, which God has promised to those who love Him.*(NKJV)" God keeps His promises. The Promise Keepers ministry employs that very characteristic of our faithful God: God keeps His promises. By putting your faith in God who loves you through fellowship with Him, what more encouragement would you need to believe in God who keeps His word?

Keep your own faith in God who loves you so much. Step out into a faithful endeavor in which you can invite God to accomplish His perfect will for whatever you're praying. Navigate with the *GPS* signal that is always accessible. Look up to see the perfect eyes of Jesus, presenting you perfectly to the Father (Jude 24). Satisfy your hunger for truthful joy by consuming God's perfect word to give back to Him, to perform it in someone's life. Stave off the lies of the enemy. Leave all crud at the cross. Always ask the Lord God for His Holy Spirit. "May the God of hope fill you with all joy and peace in believing, so that by the power of the Holy Spirit you may abound in hope" (Rom. 15:13 NKJV).

Knowing the Voice of God, listening to the direction He is suggesting, only comes through fellowship with Him. The apostle Paul didn't know God's voice when he was called. *Acts 9:4–6* (NKJV) states: "He fell to the ground and heard a voice say to him, 'Saul, Saul, why do you persecute me?' 'Who are you, Lord?' Saul asked. 'I am Jesus, whom you are persecuting.'" In his zealotry for the tradition of the fathers and not in the communion with God, Saul didn't recognize God's voice. Faith has to have a relational base from which to leap. You have to know who you believe in and to whom you want to listen. "'I am the good shepherd,' Jesus continued, 'and the *sheep* follow the shepherd because they *know his voice*. But they will never follow a stranger; in fact, they will run away from him because they do not recognize a stranger's voice'" (John 10:27; 10:5 NKJV).

Encouragingly, I pray that you take a meticulous look into the perfect word of God and meditate on learning the true voice of God, whereby you enable your faith to be strong and effective. As Paul prayed, so do I: "... that you may be *filled* with all the *fullness of God*" (Eph. 3:19 NKJV). Be encouraged; believe! The God of Hosts and the Almighty Lord, whose plan prevailed in my attempt to hike the Pacific Crest Trail, loves me and trusts me to share what I've learned. He has enlightened the eyes of my understanding and revealed how much He loves you!

I would certainly hope this actually encourages somebody to get out there and hike the Pacific Crest Trail! Inasmuch as I got distracted and forsook the PCT, not finishing it and not having the satisfactory reward of knowing I endured to get to the Canadian border, I learned that being distracted and forsaking a So-Mighty-God Who loves us, separates us from our true purpose, to be complete in, and within, Jesus our Redeemer. I still daydream about what I missed and find myself feeling kinda regretful at times (just ever so momentarily). Don't let discontent or distraction become the regret that could last eternally (looking away from God's completeness of you and hanging your head low in That Day). The Trail is good! It's beautiful! It's worth starting and sticking with it until it is completed! Get out there and discover the awesomeness of the Pacific Crest Trail! Even more so, obtain and embrace the true desire for our contentment that God will be faithful to His Word. He *is* entirely what all life is. Believe Him!

Without that first step, you can't hike the trail. Take that first step of faith in God who so loves you, so you can enjoy and believe with confidence that you will achieve the goal and the upward calling of Jesus Christ. "Brethren, I do not regard myself as having laid hold of it yet, but I press on toward the *goal* for the prize of the *upward call* of God in *Christ Jesus*" (Phil. 3:14 NASB).

What I learned from my experience on the Pacific Crest Trail is: Stay on God's trail.

God loves you that much!

www.ingramcontent.com/pod-product-compliance
Lightning Source LLC
Chambersburg PA
CBHW032047290426
44110CB00012B/996